CLOSURE IS A LIE

A Brutally Honest Reality Check About Heartbreak, Ego, and Finally Moving On

S.T. WILDER

First Edition

ISBN: 979-8-9944760-2-4

Printed in USA

CONTENTS

Author's Note

I AM NOT A therapist.

I am not a relationship guru.
I am a woman who once zoomed into Instagram stories like she was preparing evidence for court.

This book is what happens when you survive your own dramatic era.

It's what happens when you stop calling anxiety "chemistry," stop confusing inconsistency with mystery, and stop pretending mixed signals are depth.

Everything in here is lived.
Some of it is embarrassing.
Most of it is funny now.
All of it is real.

But this isn't a clean, linear story.

Some pages sound like I've figured everything out.
Others sound like I might text him back.

Both are true.

Because healing doesn't happen in a straight line.
It loops. It repeats. It humbles you.
And sometimes... it makes you laugh at things that used to break you.

I didn't write this because I have it all figured out.
I wrote it because one day I realized I was no longer heartbroken —
just aware.

Aware of what I tolerated.
Aware of what I romanticized.
Aware that chaos was never love.

This isn't about revenge.
It's not about being cold.
It's about upgrading without announcing it.

If you're ready to retire the version of you
that tolerated confusion...

welcome.

Respectfully,
S.T. Wilder

CHAPTER 1
2:17 A.M. AND NO ONE COMING BACK

ALWAYS THOUGHT HEARTBREAK would be obvious.

Crying on the floor.
Not eating.
Some dramatic moment where everything explodes and at least makes
sense.
Instead, it was just me at **2:17 a.m.**,
staring at a phone that wasn't lighting up,
refreshing nothing,
like an idiot hoping silence had changed its mind.

No message.
No explanation.
No "hey, I'm sorry."
Nothing.

Just this quiet, ugly realization that
you were probably sleeping perfectly fine
while my brain was running a full investigation on
on every conversation we ever had.

And honestly?
That part hurt more than you leaving.
Because leaving is one thing.
But leaving **and sleeping peacefully**?
That's a different level of disrespect.

Nobody really prepares you for this version of heartbreak.
Not the crying.
Not the sad songs.
Not the inspirational garbage that suddenly floods your timeline.

I mean the moment you realize
you were the only one taking any of it seriously.
The moment you understand
you weren't in a complicated love story...
You were just **more invested than the other person.**
And somehow,
you're the one who ends up feeling stupid for it.

What I still can't wrap my head around is this:
At some point,
the story flipped.

Suddenly **I** was the one who was supposed to chase.
Fight harder.
Prove more.
Convince someone to stay
who was already mentally gone.

And I remember thinking—
What the hell am I even auditioning for right now?
Girlfriend?
Wife?

Basic human respect?

Because love isn't supposed to feel like
you're begging someone
to do the bare minimum
without acting like it's a favor.

Here's the truth no one likes to admit:
I didn't collapse.
I didn't stop functioning.
I didn't become the tragic movie version of heartbreak.
I just kept living...
with this quiet, humiliating question
sitting in my chest every single day:

**How did I love someone
who could walk away this easily
and still sleep like nothing happened?**

And the worst part?
Not the silence.
Not even the leaving.
The worst part was realizing
I was still hoping
you'd come back and prove
I hadn't completely imagined
what we were.
Yeah.
That's the embarrassing part nobody posts about.
Not the sadness.
The **ego hit** of loving someone
who clearly decided
you were replaceable.

And I think that's the exact moment
something inside me changed.
Not loudly.
Not dramatically.
Just quietly enough to be dangerous.
Because once you see that kind of truth,
you can't really unsee it.

And whether I liked it or not,
that night was the beginning of learning
something I never wanted to learn in the first place:

Closure isn't something they give you.
It's something you build
after they show you exactly who they are.

CHAPTER 2

WATCHING YOUR NAME NOT SHOW UP

THERE'S A VERY SPECIFIC kind of silence that only exists after someone leaves you.

Not the peaceful kind.
Not the healing, self-love, light-a-candle,
drink-water-and-journal kind.

I mean the **stupid, obsessive kind** where you check your phone even though you already know nothing new is there.

And you still check again. Because apparently humiliation also has muscle memory.

Nobody talks about how incredibly **dumb** heartbreak makes you feel.

Not weak. Not broken.

Just... dumb.

Like refreshing the same empty screen might somehow produce a different outcome if you stare at it long enough.

Like silence is going to panic and suddenly text you back.

Spoiler: it does not.

And the worst part isn't even the checking.

It's that tiny, embarrassing piece of hope sitting in your chest like it pays rent, whispering:

Maybe they're just busy. Maybe they'll text tomorrow. Maybe this isn't what it looks like.

Hope is honestly a little delusional. Sweet, but delusional.
Because deep down, you already know the truth.

And the truth is painfully simple:
If someone wants to talk to you, they talk to you.
No mystery. No strategy. No emotional chess game.
Just effort. Or the very obvious lack of it.

I wish I could say I handled that realization with dignity.

I did not.
I checked my phone like it was a life-support machine.
Morning. Afternoon. Middle of the night when absolutely no good decisions are made.
Each time hoping this would be the moment your name showed up again like nothing had happened.
Which, in hindsight, is slightly pathetic... but also painfully human.

So we'll call it a draw.
And somewhere in the middle of all that, a quieter thought started creeping in.
Not loud. Not dramatic. Just honest in the most annoying way possible:

Why am I waiting for someone who clearly isn't waiting for me?
Yeah. That question ruins a lot of fantasies very quickly.

I DIDN'T JUST CHECK my phone.

Let's be honest.
I conducted a full-time investigation.

Sleep? Optional.
Dignity? Missing in action.

At **3:12 a.m.** I wasn't resting peacefully like a stable person. I was refreshing social media like the FBI might suddenly release emotional evidence.

Stories. Locations. Online status. Tiny digital clues that apparently felt more important than my actual mental health.

Very healthy behavior. Highly recommend. Ten out of ten for personal growth.

And every new post felt like a tiny, unnecessary insult.

Not dramatic. Just... casual happiness.

Smiling. Living. Moving on like our entire relationship was a minor scheduling conflict.

Which is a special kind of psychological experience, by the way—watching someone look completely fine while you're trying to remember how breathing used to feel normal.

But the sentence that really stayed with me wasn't on social media.

It was simple. Clean. Almost impressive in its emotional efficiency:

"I didn't think about you."

Not once. Not a little. Not sometimes.

Just... nothing.

And I remember sitting there thinking—

Wow. That's incredible.

Not in a good way. More in a **"human emotions are terrifying"** kind of way.

Because how do you go from mattering to someone... to being absolutely irrelevant in what feels like five minutes?

How does your face, your voice, your entire existence just... disappear from someone's emotional world like you were never there?

I genuinely wanted to understand.

Not to fix it. Not to change it.

Just to know **how that's even possible.**

And maybe that's the real heartbreak nobody explains.

Not losing the person.

Losing the **meaning** you thought you had in their life.

Because grief is one thing. But realizing you might be completely forgettable?

Yeah. That hits a little different.

I kept asking myself the same question in a hundred slightly more dramatic versions:

Was any of it real to you? Or was I just... convenient at the time?

Very calm thoughts. Super emotionally balanced. No notes.

And somewhere between no sleep, too much scrolling, and conversations with myself that absolutely should have been billed as therapy...

another quieter thought showed up.

Annoying. Uninvited. Unfortunately logical.

If someone can lose you and feel nothing...

then maybe the real question isn't why they moved on so fast.

Maybe it's **why you were fighting so hard to stay somewhere you clearly weren't being held.**

I didn't like that thought.

Didn't agree with it. Tried to emotionally block it. Would not recommend.

But it stayed anyway.

Because truth has this irritating habit of showing up right when denial is getting comfortable.

And that was the moment the silence stopped feeling confusing...
and started feeling like an answer.

Not a nice one. Not a fair one. Definitely not the one I wanted.
But clear.
Painfully, stupidly clear.

You weren't coming back. And worse— you didn't even miss leaving.

Type it. Don't send it.

CHAPTER 3

The Embarrassing Things I Called Love

THERE'S A VERY UNCOMFORTABLE stage of heartbreak that nobody advertises.

Not the crying. Not the stalking. We've already established I was thriving in both.

I mean the part where your **memory starts cooperating** and suddenly begins replaying moments you previously labeled as:

- "not a big deal"

- "just stress"

- "he didn't mean it like that"

Which is adorable in hindsight. Truly. Gold medal performance in **emotional denial.**

Because once the silence drags on long enough, your brain—which has apparently been waiting for permission—starts pulling up receipts.

Unsolicited. Detailed. Rude in timing.

And you begin remembering things that felt small back then but now look... suspiciously like **red flags wearing good lighting.**

Like the way I kept explaining your behavior to other people as if I worked in **customer service for your personality.**

"Oh, he's just tired." "He's under pressure." "He doesn't mean it."

Meanwhile, the bare minimum was being treated like a **premium luxury service** I should feel grateful to receive.

Romantic. Really.

And at some point, a very offensive thought entered my brain:

What if this wasn't complicated? What if it was just... bad?

I know. Radical theory.

Because love, real love, probably isn't supposed to feel like:

- constant confusion

- emotional guessing games

- begging for basic consistency

- celebrating crumbs like they're full meals

Just a wild hypothesis. Still waiting on peer review.

And here's the truly humbling part:

I didn't just tolerate it. I **defended** it.

Which means the person who hurt me wasn't the only one not protecting my peace.

Yeah. That realization deserved a moment of silence too.

Something inside me started shifting here. Not healing. Let's not get inspirational.

More like... **my ego slowly sitting up in bed** looking around and whispering:

"We accepted *what*, exactly?"

Embarrassing question. Valid question. Late question... but we'll take the progress.

ONCE YOUR MEMORY STARTS cooperating, things get uncomfortable very quickly.

Because suddenly you're not just remembering the good moments.

You're remembering the **weird ones**. The ones you explained away in real time like a public relations manager for someone who was absolutely not paying you.

And the more honest the memories get, the more one very rude question keeps showing up:

Why did I tolerate that?

Not once. Not twice. But repeatedly. With enthusiasm.

Which is honestly impressive from a psychological standpoint.

I used to think love meant:

- patience

- understanding

- giving people grace

- seeing the best in them

All beautiful ideas. Very mature. **Ten out of ten emotionally.**

Unfortunately, I also used those same ideas to justify behavior that should have come with a **warning label**.

Because there's a thin line between being loving and being **in denial with good intentions**.

And I crossed that line like it wasn't even there.

Looking back, the red flags weren't subtle.

They were practically doing choreography in front of me.

And I still stood there thinking:

Maybe this is just... modern love?

Which is a sentence I would like to formally apologize for.

There were moments that should have made me pause.

Moments that should have made me ask:

"Is this actually healthy?"

Instead, I asked:

"How can I fix this?"

Classic mistake. Timeless, really. Women everywhere deserve a group discount for therapy.

And here's the most humbling realization of all:

I wasn't confused because the situation was complicated.

I was confused because the truth was **simple** and I didn't want to see it.

Simple truths are rude like that. No poetry. No mystery. Just clarity you specifically didn't order.

At some point, the sadness started mixing with something else.

Not strength. Let's not get inspirational too fast.

More like... **mild embarrassment waking up slowly.**

The kind where you look back and think:

"Wow. I really gave 110% to someone giving... emotional buffering."

Very athletic of me. Wrong sport, but still.

And the first time I laughed at myself a little— not in a cruel way, just in a tired, honest way— I realized something important:

Maybe healing doesn't start with becoming strong.

Maybe it starts with finally admitting:

"Okay... that was a little ridiculous."

Not the love. Love is never ridiculous.

But the **things I accepted in the name of love?**

Yeah. We can laugh at those. Gently. With respect. And maybe a little disbelief.

Because once you can laugh—even a tiny bit—something shifts.

Not everything. Not instantly.

But enough to know you won't abandon yourself like that again.

And honestly?

That's the first real sign that the story is changing.

Chapter 4

Hope Without Evidence

THERE'S A SPECIAL KIND of confidence that only shows up in hindsight. The kind where you look back at a situation and think, *wow... I really ignored everything, didn't I?*

Not one red flag. Not two. **An entire parade — with music, lights, and probably backup dancers** — and I was still standing there telling myself he was just stressed. Incredible emotional strategy. Truly groundbreaking.

The truth is, the signs were never confusing. They were just inconvenient. And inconvenient truths are remarkably easy to ignore when you're emotionally invested in the ending. Seeing clearly would have meant making a decision, and making a decision would have meant risking the loss. So instead, I chose something far more comfortable: hope without evidence.

I didn't just overlook the signs. I explained them, softened them, and quietly rearranged reality so the story could still work. Emotional distance became *"he needs space. "* Inconsistency became *"he's overwhelmed. "* The bare minimum somehow turned into something I should feel grateful to receive. Looking back, the level of creativity alone deserves recognition.

And the most humbling part is that, somewhere underneath all the explaining, I already knew something wasn't right. Not in a loud, dramatic way. Just a small, persistent discomfort that kept trying to get my attention. The kind you talk yourself out of because the alternative is admitting the person you love might not choose you the same way.

That quiet knowing is easy to ignore in the moment. In hindsight, it's impossible to miss.

The strangest part of looking back isn't the red flags themselves. It's how normal they felt at the time.

Not good. Not healthy. Just... familiar enough to tolerate.

And tolerance is a dangerous thing when it shows up dressed like loyalty. Because you tell yourself you're being patient, understanding, mature — all the words that make staying feel noble instead of quietly self-abandoning.

I thought I was fighting for love. In reality, I was mostly fighting **reality**.

Which, to be fair, is a difficult opponent. Very consistent. Rarely negotiates.

There's a moment that happens in hindsight when the whole story rearranges itself.

Nothing new occurs. No dramatic confession. No cinematic ending.

You just finally see the same memories without trying to protect the person in them.

And suddenly things look... different.

Clearer. Colder. A little embarrassing, if we're being honest.

Because once you remove hope from the equation, a lot of behavior loses its charm.

Mystery becomes avoidance. Space becomes distance. Confusion becomes disinterest.

It's amazing how romantic something can feel right up until the moment you tell the truth about it.

And here's the part that stings a little, but also sets you free in a quiet way:

I wasn't confused because he was complicated. I was confused because I **wanted a different answer.**

That's a humbling realization. Not devastating. Just... humbling enough to sit with for a minute and maybe laugh a little at the version of me who kept trying to win a game no one else was playing.

She meant well. She really did. Terrible strategy, though.

The shift didn't feel powerful. No sudden confidence. No dramatic "I'm done" speech in the mirror.
Just a small, steady awareness that kept getting harder to ignore:
If someone has to be convinced to love you correctly, they probably don't.
Simple. Uninspiring. Extremely useful information.
And strangely, that truth wasn't as painful as all the hoping had been.
Because hope can stretch suffering far longer than reality ever could.
Reality just says, *"This is what it is. "*
Hope says, *"Maybe tomorrow will be different."* for six more months.

Very generous. Completely exhausting.

So no, I didn't become strong overnight. I didn't suddenly stop caring. I didn't walk away like a movie character with perfect lighting and emotional closure.
I just got a little more honest. And honesty, it turns out, is much quieter than heartbreak —but a lot more stable.

And maybe that was the real beginning. Not healing. Not happiness. Just the moment I stopped rewriting the story to make someone else look better in it.
A small change. But an important one.
Because once you stop lying to yourself, you don't actually need closure anymore.
You just need distance... and a little self-respect that finally decided to wake up.
Late, yes. But right on time.

CHAPTER 5

The Exact Moment I Realized You Were Fine Without Me

THE MOMENT I REALIZED he was fine without me wasn't dramatic. There was no emotional crescendo, no cinematic clarity where everything suddenly made sense. It happened on a completely ordinary day, which somehow made it worse. You expect heartbreak to at least respect your suffering enough to be theatrical. Instead, it shows up casually, like it forgot you were still grieving.

For weeks, I had been telling myself very reasonable stories. Mature stories. The kind that make you feel emotionally intelligent while you're actually negotiating with reality. He just needs space. He's overwhelmed. He's processing everything. He'll come back when he realizes what we had. I packaged those thoughts carefully, like they were facts.

They weren't facts.

They were hope dressed up in business casual.

If I'm honest, the signs weren't subtle. They weren't layered or complicated. **At one point, I'm fairly certain the universe sent me a PowerPoint presentation.**

Slide one: He's not coming back. Slide two: He's sleeping peacefully. Slide three: You are ignoring all available data.

And I still clicked **"remind me later."**

The loyalty? Impressive. The direction? Catastrophic.

I told myself I didn't care. Which is fascinating, because I had refreshed his story so many times **Instagram probably assumed I was on payroll. I** wasn't stalking. I was observing. Monitoring. Conducting light research. If heartbreak offered certifications, I would have graduated with honors in Digital Surveillance.

I checked Snap Maps like I was preparing a legal case. Zoomed in. Zoomed out. Interpreted timestamps with unnecessary seriousness.
Exhibit A: Active 14 minutes ago. Exhibit B: Laughing publicly. Exhibit C: Me, spiraling privately.

The thing about checking is that it never brings peace. It only brings more material. A new follow. A new like. A new laugh in a video. And nothing destabilizes you quite like watching someone laugh easily after leaving you. Not a forced laugh. Not a coping laugh. A real one. Effortless. Light. Free.

There's something deeply offensive about that level of ease.
Because while I was mentally replaying every conversation we ever had, he was simply living. Not conflicted. Not tortured. Not one realization away from returning. Just fine.

That's when the ego steps in, and the ego is not gentle.
Sadness is expected. Ego is humiliating.

You start asking questions that don't feel good in your mouth. How does someone go from loving you to not thinking about you at all? How do you switch that cleanly? Was I dramatic? Was I replaceable? Was I just convenient?

And then the uncomfortable one: was I the only one who thought this was permanent?

I tried to perform indifference. It was my best role. "I'm good." "I'm fine." "It is what it is." Meanwhile, I hadn't slept properly in days. I would wake up at 3:14 a. m. — because heartbreak enjoys symbolic timing — and immediately reach for my phone like it was oxygen.

Maybe he texted.
He didn't.
Maybe he posted something sad.
He didn't.
Maybe he slipped and revealed he missed me.
He did not.
Remarkable consistency.

There's a strange phase where you pretend not to care, but care aggressively. Quietly. Internally. With discipline. You don't beg. You don't send paragraphs. You don't embarrass yourself publicly. You just unravel privately while maintaining composure like it's a competitive sport.

I reanalyzed old messages like they contained prophecy. "He said he was tired." What kind of tired? Emotional fatigue? Existential dread? A coded warning I ignored? No. He was probably just tired. But that interpretation didn't support the narrative, so I kept digging.

The turning point wasn't when I stopped checking. It was when I realized checking changed nothing. He was still living. Still moving. Still smiling in ways that did not include me.

And that's when it landed — not violently, not dramatically — just clearly.

He was fine without me.
Not pretending. Not suppressing. Not secretly unraveling at night.

Fine.

And that word should be illegal after a breakup.

Because once you accept that someone is fine without you, something sharp happens. Fantasy dissolves. Denial packs up quietly. And you're left with the simplest, most inconvenient truth: they chose that.

You cannot compete with someone's choice. Trying only turns you into a contestant on a show you never auditioned for — where the prize is a man who already left.

That realization didn't make me powerful overnight. It didn't restore my pride in a single moment. It just made me honest. And honesty is quieter than heartbreak, but far more stable.

The question shifted. It stopped being "Why wasn't I enough?" and became something far less flattering to my ego:

Why was I trying so hard to be enough for someone who wasn't trying at all?

That question didn't feel empowering. It felt exposing. But it also felt solid. And solid is better than hopeful.

The exact moment I realized he was fine without me wasn't the end of the pain. It was the end of pretending.

And once pretending ends, you don't explode.
You straighten your spine.
You close the tabs.
And you stop competing.
Not because you don't care.
But because you finally understand you don't need to.

Chapter 6

The Bare Minimum Is Not A Love Language

NEED TO START this chapter by asking myself something mildly humiliating.

What exactly was I applauding?
Not metaphorically. Not poetically. Specifically.
What behavior did I look at and decide. *yes. this is premium?*

Because at some point. I convinced myself that effort meant something it didn't. That showing up occasionally was devotion. That replying eventually was romance. That not actively disrespecting me counted as character development.

The bar wasn't low.
It was underground.
And I brought a shovel.

I used to describe him as "not that bad." which is a remarkable standard for someone you're supposedly building a life with. Not that bad is something you say about airline food. It is not the foundation of emotional security.

But I said it with conviction.

"He tries." "He's just guarded." "He struggles with emotions."
Struggles with emotions.

As if emotional availability were an elective class he just hadn't gotten around to taking.

The truth is. I mistook potential for partnership. I saw who he could be and treated it like who he already was. I graded effort on a curve so steep it required imagination.
He texted back eventually. He apologized sometimes. He said he cared.
And I filled in the rest.
That's the part that stings.

Because the bare minimum only looks like effort when you're hungry for reassurance. And I was hungry. Not for attention — for steadiness. For someone whose affection didn't feel conditional on mood. timing. or convenience.
Instead of asking why I felt unsettled so often. I asked how I could be easier to love.

That's where the self-roast really begins.
I softened my reactions. I minimized my standards. I convinced myself that asking for consistency was dramatic. I treated basic emotional reliability like it was a luxury feature instead of standard equipment.

He didn't promise the moon. He didn't even promise the driveway.
He promised vague future energy and selective presence. And I called it commitment.

Creative. Very creative.

He wasn't malicious. He wasn't plotting. He wasn't calculating how little he could give to keep me interested. He was operating exactly at his capacity.
And I kept adjusting mine.
That's the uncomfortable truth.

The bare minimum is not a love language. It's a maintenance setting — and I was calling it luxury.

He would show up sometimes. He would reassure me occasionally. He would be warm when it suited him.
And I clapped like it was a standing ovation.
That's the shift. Not rage. Not revenge.
Recognition.

The moment you realize you weren't asking for too much — you were asking the wrong person.
There's a difference.
And once you see it. you can't unsee it.

I used to think love meant patience. And it does — but not silent shrinking. Not emotional overfunctioning. Not applauding someone for doing what adults are already supposed to do.

The most humbling realization wasn't that he gave the bare minimum.

It was that I accepted it.
That's growth.
Not dramatic. Not explosive.
Just... upgraded standards.

CHAPTER 7

So Apparently, I Have a Type

THERE IS A VERY specific moment in every woman's life when she looks at her relationship history and thinks, respectfully... this feels familiar. Different face. Different voice. Same emotional layout.

At some point, I had to admit something mildly inconvenient.

It wasn't just him.

It was a pattern.

And patterns are much harder to be mad at, because patterns include you.

I used to say, "I just attract emotionally unavailable men."

Which sounds poetic. Slightly tragic. Almost mysterious.

It's also incomplete.

Because attraction is rarely accidental. We don't just stumble into the same dynamic repeatedly by coincidence. We walk into it with recognition.

Comfortable recognition.

And that's the part that stings.

There was something about men who were a little distant, a little complicated, a little hard to fully reach that felt familiar. Not exciting — familiar. Like a challenge I already understood.

He wasn't overly affectionate. He wasn't wildly expressive. He wasn't flooding me with security.

He made me earn steadiness.

And for some reason, that felt like love.

That's the pattern.

Not that they were emotionally unavailable.

But that I was comfortable chasing availability.

There's a difference.

Emotionally consistent men didn't always feel intense to me. They felt… stable. Calm. Predictable.

And I confused predictable with boring.

That one hurts to admit.

Because intensity is addictive. The highs feel high. The reconnecting feels dramatic. The temporary closeness after distance feels electric.

But electric isn't stable.

It's just loud.

And I had been mistaking loud for meaningful.

When someone pulls away slightly, and you lean in harder — that's not chemistry. That's conditioning.

And I was very well conditioned.

I didn't fall for chaos because I liked chaos. I fell for it because it felt like something I knew how to navigate. I knew how to overgive. I knew how to soften. I knew how to explain someone's behavior in a way that made them look better than it felt.

That skill? Impressive.

Misapplied.

I used to think being patient meant I was emotionally mature. Sometimes it did. Sometimes it meant I was tolerating things I shouldn't have.

There's a thin line between understanding someone and excusing them.

I blurred it beautifully.

And here's the uncomfortable part.

There was something validating about being chosen by someone who didn't choose easily.

If he finally opened up to me, I must be special. If he let his guard down with me, I must have earned it. If he picked me despite being emotionally reserved, that must mean something deeper.

Or it meant he felt safe enough in that moment.

Which is lovely.

But safety is not commitment.

And effort given in flashes is not stability.

I didn't have a type.

I had a comfort zone.

And my comfort zone required me to prove myself.

That realization is quieter than heartbreak, but heavier.

Because you can't be angry at a pattern without also examining the part of you that keeps participating.

That's where growth starts.

Not in blaming them.

In recognizing what feels familiar — and asking why.

There's something dangerously flattering about being chosen by someone who doesn't choose easily.

It feels earned.

If he finally opens up to you, you must be different. If he lets his guard down just a little, that must mean you reached somewhere no one else could. If he's distant with everyone but soft with you sometimes, that must mean you're special.

Or it means he was comfortable in that moment.

And comfort is not exclusivity.

But when someone who withholds finally gives, even briefly, it feels
amplified. The small gestures feel significant. The minimal effort feels rare.
And rare gets mistaken for valuable.

That's how intensity tricks you.

It's not the consistency that feels exciting. It's the unpredictability. The
distance followed by closeness. The pullback followed by reassurance. The
moment you think you're losing him — and then he leans in again.

That swing creates adrenaline.

Adrenaline is not intimacy.

It's just loud.

And loud feels like something is happening.

I used to think those emotional highs meant depth. That if something felt
intense, it must be meaningful. Calm felt suspicious. Stable felt flat. Predictable
felt like the beginning of boredom.

That's not romance. That's nervous system confusion.

But at the time, it felt like chemistry.

There's also an ego element we don't talk about enough. Being chosen by
someone who isn't easy to get feels validating. It feels like you passed a test no
one else could. Like you cracked a code.

He doesn't open up easily. But he opened up to me.

It sounds romantic.

It's also a competition you didn't realize you entered.

Because once you frame love as something you win, you start performing.
You soften more. You explain more. You accept more. You become
accommodating in ways that feel noble but are actually strategic.

You're not just loving.

You're maintaining your position.

And that's exhausting.

I didn't just want to be loved. I wanted to be the exception. The one who got through. The one who made him different. The one who unlocked him.

That desire? Honest.

Also slightly delusional.

Because you cannot unlock someone who does not want to open.

And if you have to earn consistency, it isn't consistency.

Looking back, I don't think I was addicted to emotionally unavailable men.

I think I was addicted to the feeling of being chosen by them.

And that's a much harder pattern to confront.

Because that's not about them.

That's about identity.

Who am I if I'm not the woman who fixes, softens, understands, and waits?

That question doesn't explode.

It lingers.

And once you sit with it long enough, something shifts.

Intensity starts to look unstable instead of romantic.

Distance starts to look like information instead of mystery.

And suddenly, calm doesn't feel boring.

It feels safe.

That's new.

And new feels unfamiliar.

But unfamiliar isn't wrong.

Sometimes it's growth.

If I'm honest, this pattern didn't start with him.

That's not dramatic. It's just factual.

There was something familiar about loving someone slightly out of reach. Something that felt earned rather than freely given. I don't need to unpack my entire childhood to admit that being chosen has always felt powerful to me. Being steady didn't feel powerful. Being needed did.

There's a difference.

When love feels like something you win, you start performing without realizing it. You adjust your tone. You shrink your reactions. You soften your standards. Not because you're weak — but because you're invested.

And investment can blur your vision.

It's easier to believe someone is "complex" than to admit they're inconsistent. It's easier to call distance "depth" than to call it disinterest. It's easier to frame unpredictability as passion than to admit it makes you anxious.

But once you see the pattern, it loses some of its glamour.
Intensity stops looking romantic.
It starts looking unstable.

And calm — the thing I used to label boring — begins to look like peace.

That's the shift.
Not loud. Not dramatic.
Just clarity.
I didn't have bad luck.
I had a preference I hadn't questioned.

And once you question it, you don't go back to calling chaos chemistry.

You recognize it for what it is.

Information.

CHAPTER 8

WHEN HE SAID I SHOULD'VE FOUGHT FOR HIM

W HEN HE SAID I should have fought for him, I didn't yell.

I didn't argue.

I didn't defend myself.

I just stared at him for a second, trying to understand what exactly I was supposed to be fighting for.

You left.

And now I'm supposed to chase you?

That felt backwards.

Not emotionally — structurally.

There's something disorienting about being told you didn't try hard enough by the person who walked away. It shifts the narrative in a way that makes you question your own memory. Was I passive? Did I not show up? Did I not care enough?

So I replayed it calmly.

I showed up. I stayed. I explained. I adjusted. I softened.

At what point does "fighting" become begging?

That's the line I couldn't cross.

We were sitting across from each other — not dramatic, not explosive — just tired. The kind of tired that happens after too many circular conversations. He said it almost casually, like it was an obvious conclusion.

"You didn't fight for me."

And something inside me went very still.
Because I had fought. I fought by staying when it was uncomfortable. I fought by having conversations I didn't enjoy. I fought by trying to understand distance instead of reacting to it. I fought by managing my own emotions so the situation wouldn't escalate.
What I didn't do was chase someone who was already stepping away.

Apparently, that was the fight he meant.
There's a quiet expectation in some relationships that if one person pulls back, the other should lean in harder. Prove loyalty. Prove desire. Prove they won't let go easily.

But pursuit feels very different depending on who is doing it.

When a man pursues, it's romantic.
When a woman pursues someone who is actively leaving, it feels like self-abandonment.
And that distinction matters.
I wasn't unwilling to fight.
I was unwilling to perform for someone who had already chosen distance.
There's a difference.

I don't think he was malicious. I don't think he was plotting. I think he genuinely believed that if I loved him enough, I would have chased harder.
But love and pursuit are not the same thing.

If I had called more, cried louder, sent longer paragraphs explaining my devotion, maybe he would have felt chosen. Maybe his ego would have softened. Maybe it would have looked like effort.

But at what cost?

Because at some point, "fighting" becomes one-sided endurance.

And I had already endured.

I endured the mixed signals. The warmth followed by distance. The moments of reassurance that never quite settled into stability. The unspoken expectation that I should lean in when he leaned out.

That dynamic creates a loop. One person withdraws slightly. The other compensates. The withdrawal increases. The compensation grows. Eventually one person feels pursued and the other feels exhausted.

And then somehow, the exhausted one is told they didn't try hard enough.

That's where ego quietly enters the room.

Being chased feels validating. It feels powerful to know someone won't let you go easily. It reinforces importance.

But validation and partnership are not the same thing.

If someone needs you to beg in order to feel valued, that's not love.

That's ego management.

And I was no longer applying for that position.

When he said I should have fought for him, what I heard was this: you should have proven I mattered more than your pride.

But it wasn't pride.

It was self-respect.

And self-respect is inconvenient because it refuses to audition.

It doesn't chase. It doesn't negotiate. It doesn't perform dramatic monologues in parking lots at 11:47 p.m.

It stands still.

And if standing still looks cold to someone who expected pursuit, I'm comfortable with that misunderstanding.

I used to think fighting meant proving I cared more.

Now I understand it means knowing when to stop proving anything at all.
If someone needs you to beg in order to feel important, that's not romance.
That's ego management.
And I quietly resigned from that position.
You cannot build something stable while sprinting after someone who is already halfway down the block.

That's not partnership.
That's cardio — and I'm no longer training for that event.

Chapter 9

Why Did I Feel Replaceable?

THE PART THAT HURT wasn't that he left.

It was how easily he seemed to continue.

There's something quietly brutal about realizing you were deeply attached to someone who appears only mildly affected by your absence.

It makes you question the entire narrative.

Was I ever special?

Not in a dramatic way. In a logistical way.

If I mattered the way I thought I did, how does someone transition that smoothly? How do you go from "you're my person" to "you're a chapter" without visible turbulence?

That's where the ego gets loud.

Not angry.

Insecure.

Because replaceable doesn't feel like heartbreak.

It feels like humiliation.

Because once the idea of being replaceable enters your head, it doesn't knock politely.

It moves in.

I didn't just wonder if he missed me.

I wondered if I had overestimated my importance entirely.

Did I imagine the connection? Did I romanticize my role in his life? Was I meaningful — or just convenient?

Those aren't empowering questions.

They're ego questions.

And ego doesn't care about logic. It cares about ranking.

If he can move on quickly, what does that say about me?

That's the part no one likes admitting.

It wasn't just sadness.

It was comparison.

Who is she? Is she calmer? Prettier? Less complicated? More agreeable?

Did he seem lighter with her because I was heavy?

See? Not elegant thoughts.

Just honest ones.

And the worst part about comparison is that it feels like investigation, but it's actually self-sabotage.

I wasn't trying to learn anything.

I was trying to confirm a fear.

The fear wasn't that he left.

The fear was that I was easily replaced.

That maybe I was intense. Maybe I was too emotional. Maybe I asked for too much. Maybe someone simpler fit him better.

That's when your mind starts rewriting the relationship in reverse. You start downplaying your strengths. Reframing your needs as flaws. Calling your standards "pressure."

Very convenient.

Very untrue.

The ego hates feeling interchangeable.

And watching someone move on quickly feels like being downgraded without explanation.

But here's what took me longer to admit:

Replaceable is a perspective, not a fact.

You can be deeply meaningful to someone and still not be chosen long-term.

Those two things are not mutually exclusive.

Someone moving on doesn't erase what you were.

It just reveals what they were capable of sustaining.

And that shift — from "What's wrong with me?" to "What was he able to hold?" — changes everything.

It wasn't the breakup that made me spiral.

It was a photo.

Blurry. Casual. Probably insignificant.

And I zoomed in like it contained classified information.

Who is she? Is that her hand? Is he smiling differently? Does he look lighter?

There is nothing dignified about analyzing someone's facial expression at 200% zoom.

But there I was.

Trying to decode whether his happiness looked new or just recycled.

I told myself I was curious.

I was not curious.

I was auditing my replacement.

That's when the thought slipped in quietly:

Maybe I wasn't special.

Not dramatically. Not tragically.

Just logistically.

If he can replicate the connection that easily, what exactly was rare about me?

That's the ego bruise.

Because heartbreak makes you question your uniqueness. And uniqueness feels like safety. If you were irreplaceable, the story wouldn't end.

But people don't replace you.
They repeat their patterns.
And modern dating makes that repetition look glamorous.
Because now it's not just moving on. It's moving on publicly.
With filters. With captions. With "soft launch" hands in pictures. With curated mystery.
We don't just break up anymore. We rebrand.
And suddenly you're not grieving. You're competing with a highlight reel.

It used to be that you healed in private.
Now you heal while watching someone perform being fine.
And I was out here refreshing like a shareholder.
Checking updates. Monitoring story views. Looking for emotional stock fluctuations.

Respectfully, I was unhinged.
Modern dating doesn't just test your attachment. It tests your ego.
Because it's no longer just: "Did he move on?"
It's: "How does he look while doing it?"

And I was analyzing lighting like it held emotional meaning.
It did not.
And that distinction took me longer than I'd like to admit.
I wasn't interchangeable.
I was incompatible with his capacity.
And those are not the same thing.

And here's another thing that took me longer than I care to admit:
Feeling replaceable doesn't mean you are.
It means your ego is trying to protect you from rejection by rewriting the story.
Replaceable sounds smaller than incompatible.
Replaceable sounds like you lost a competition.
Incompatible sounds like the pieces simply didn't fit.

One attacks your value.
The other acknowledges capacity.

And once I understood that, something shifted.

Not loudly.
Not triumphantly.
Just quietly.
I stopped zooming in.
I stopped auditing strangers.
I stopped measuring my worth against someone else's timeline.

Because here's the inconvenient truth:
If someone can move on quickly, that says more about their attachment style than your depth.
Depth doesn't disappear.
Capacity does.
And I finally understood something that would've saved me weeks of comparison:
You are not replaceable.
You are repeatable only to someone who hasn't changed.
And I have no interest in being repeated.

CHAPTER 10
I WASN'T TOO MUCH

I SPENT AN EMBARRASSING amount of time wondering if I was exhausting.

Too emotional. Too intense. Too opinionated. Too aware.

Which is wild, considering most of what I asked for was consistency and basic communication. Apparently that's advanced-level relationship stuff now.

For a while, I genuinely tried to shrink.

Not dramatically. Subtly.

I'd pause before saying something. Rephrase things to sound softer. Delay conversations so I wouldn't seem "confrontational."

Which is hilarious, because nothing says healthy relationship like rehearsing your tone alone in your own kitchen.

The thing about being told you're too much is that you start managing yourself instead of managing the problem. You adjust your volume instead of asking why someone is allergic to depth.

And here's what I eventually realized:

I wasn't too much. I was just incompatible with someone who preferred comfort over clarity.

That's not the same thing.

Shrinking to make someone else feel secure isn't maturity.

It's slow self-erasure.

I didn't shrink dramatically. There was no announcement. No identity collapse. It was smaller than that.

I started laughing at jokes that didn't land. I stopped bringing up things that bothered me because "it's not that serious." I softened statements that didn't need softening.

Instead of saying, "That hurt," I'd say, "It's fine."

It was rarely fine.

I remember rewriting a message three times just to make sure it didn't sound "too emotional." Three drafts to say something basic. Like I was submitting a formal proposal instead of expressing a feeling.

And the worst part?

He probably didn't even notice.

That's when it hit me.

I wasn't being "too much." I was being slowly diluted.

Which is impressive, because I've never identified as sparkling water.

But there I was. Becoming flatter to avoid making waves.

You don't wake up one day tiny. You gradually adjust. Lower your standards. Lower your tone. Lower your expectations. And call it maturity.

That one stung.

Because it sounded responsible. It sounded evolved.

But really, I was just afraid that if I held my ground, I'd lose him.

And eventually I did.

Which is almost poetic.

All that shrinking.

And I still wasn't small enough to keep someone who needed less.

All that adjusting. All that calibrating. All that careful self-editing.

And I still ended up here.

Which tells you something.

You can shrink yourself to half your size and still be "too much" for someone who prefers emotional minimalism.

That's not a flaw.

That's a mismatch.

I wasn't too much. I was just asking for something he didn't know how to sustain.

And instead of calling that incompatibility, I called it self-improvement.

That's the part I won't do again.

Not louder. Not colder.

Just clearer.

If someone feels overwhelmed by clarity, that's not my volume problem.

That's their capacity.

And I'm no longer compressing myself to fit inside someone else's limitations.

CHAPTER 11

THE DAY I STOPPED COMPETING

I T DIDN'T HAPPEN IN some dramatic, cinematic way.

There was no speech. No "I deserve better" moment. No unfollow-and-glow-up montage.

It happened on a random Tuesday.

I was lying in bed, phone too close to my face, scrolling past a photo I absolutely did not need to analyze.

And I felt it.

That familiar tightening.

Not heartbreak.

Competition.

It wasn't even about him anymore. It was about her.

Was she calmer? Less intense? More agreeable? Did she laugh at things I used to question?

And the worst part?

I wasn't trying to get him back.

I was trying to win.

That realization made me sit up.

Because at some point, without realizing it, I had entered a silent contest no one officially announced.

Who is more effortless? Who is less emotional?Who needs less reassurance? Who is more "easy"?

It's exhausting to compete in a game where the prize is someone's inconsistent attention.
And here's what hit me — not dramatically, just clearly:
If I have to outperform another woman to be chosen, I've already disqualified myself.
That's not attraction.
That's auditioning.
And I don't audition for someone who isn't even offering a stable role.

That Tuesday wasn't revolutionary.
But it was honest.
I didn't feel empowered.
I felt tired.
Tired of measuring myself against women who were simply playing a different version of the same dynamic.
Tired of acting like detachment was a personality trait I needed to adopt.
Tired of pretending I didn't care so I could appear less invested.
I wasn't competing for love.
I was competing for ego validation.
And once I saw that, the game lost its appeal.
It would be easy to pretend social media has nothing to do with it.

But let's be honest.
Visibility changes behavior.
When options are constantly visible, attention becomes currency. And attention is addictive.
We don't just date people anymore.
We observe them being observed.
You can literally watch someone move on in real time.
Watch them smile in photos.
Watch new faces appear.

Watch stories that don't include you.

And suddenly heartbreak isn't private.

It's comparative.

And comparison breeds performance.

Who looks unbothered? Who looks happier? Who moved on first? Who seems lighter?

We start curating our own reactions.

Posting strategically. Staying quiet strategically. Appearing fine strategically.

It's exhausting.

And here's the uncomfortable part:

Being chased feels good.

For anyone.

Male ego isn't uniquely flawed.

It's human.

If someone pulls away and you lean in harder, that pursuit creates a power imbalance. And power feels validating.

But validation isn't stability.

It's stimulation.

And social media amplifies that dynamic.

The more visible your options, the more valuable attention feels.

So instead of building something steady, people build intrigue.

Instead of clarity, they build ambiguity.

Instead of commitment, they build competition.

And for a while, I played along.

I pretended I didn't care. I posted like I was thriving. I tried to appear less affected than I was.

Not because I wanted him back.

But because I didn't want to look replaceable.

That's when I realized something quietly sobering:

If I have to outperform someone else to feel chosen, I am not building a relationship.

I am building a résumé.
And I'm not applying for a role that expires when someone new walks into frame.
At some point, the competition stopped feeling dramatic.
It started feeling unstable.

Because the moment you realize you're adjusting yourself in response to someone else's attention shifts, you understand something important:
You're not building anything solid.
You're reacting.
And reacting is exhausting.
If someone's interest depends on how well you perform detachment, or how effortlessly you appear, or how convincingly you seem unbothered — that's not chemistry.
That's instability disguised as attraction.
The constant comparing, posting, withholding, analyzing — it wasn't empowering.

It was fragile.
And fragile dynamics require constant maintenance.
I don't want maintenance.
I want stability.
And stability doesn't compete.
It doesn't scan the room for alternatives.
It doesn't need to win.
It chooses.
Quietly.
Consistently.
Without spectacle.

The day I stopped competing wasn't dramatic.
I didn't block anyone.
I didn't announce anything.

I just stopped measuring myself against strangers and started measuring the dynamic instead.

And once I saw it clearly, the competition felt unnecessary.
Not because I was better.
Because I was done building on something that required constant proof.

At some point, I realized something slightly humiliating: I was interviewing for roles that were never officially offered.

Girlfriend. Future. Priority. Stability.
And I was submitting my résumé emotionally.

It wasn't obvious at first. It didn't look like desperation. It looked like effort. I was attentive. Understanding. Flexible. I framed it as being "emotionally mature." But underneath all of that was a quiet assumption that I needed to prove I was worth choosing.

Look how calm I stay when you pull away. Look how understanding I am when plans change. Look how low-maintenance I can be.

I wasn't dating.

I was auditioning.

And auditioning puts someone else in casting control. They evaluate. They decide. They reward. Without saying it out loud, you start adjusting yourself to increase your chances of being selected.

You soften opinions. You delay responses strategically. You pretend not to notice shifts in tone. You tell yourself you're being patient when you're actually being nervous.

I once waited three hours to reply to a message just to seem "busy."

I was not busy.

I was calculating.

Nothing screams secure attachment like strategic texting delays.

The problem with auditioning is that it quietly assumes the power lives outside of you. That someone else gets to determine whether you qualify for stability. And once you start operating that way, you stop evaluating them.

You focus on being chosen instead of asking, "Do I even like this dynamic?"

That shift is subtle, but it changes everything.

Because the moment you stop auditioning, you stop performing.

And the moment you stop performing, you see clearly.

If someone needs to be convinced of your value, they are not offering partnership.

They're offering a stage.

And I'm not here to perform.

CHAPTER 12

I HAD WI-FI AND TOO MUCH IMAGINATION

THERE WAS A VERSION of me that should not have had internet access.

Not because I was dramatic.

Because I was creative.

Heartbreak plus imagination plus unlimited Wi-Fi is not a healthy combination.

I wasn't just sad.

I was investigative.

I didn't spiral. I conducted research.

At one point, I checked Snapchat maps like it was a government tracking system.

Oh, he's at that bar again?

Interesting.

Interesting for absolutely no reason.

I zoomed into Instagram stories like I was enhancing security footage.

Is that a female laugh in the background?

Pause. Rewind. Pause again.

Respectfully, I was unwell.

But in my defense, heartbreak turns normal women into emotional analysts.

You start reading three-word texts like they're encrypted messages.
"Okay."
What do you mean okay?
Is it annoyed okay? Detached okay? Moving-on okay?
Smiling-at-someone-else-while-texting-me okay?

I once spent fifteen minutes interpreting punctuation.
He used a period.
A period.
That must mean something.
It did not mean something.
It meant he used a period.

The wildest part?
I would tell myself I wasn't checking.
I was just "happening to see."
I wasn't stalking.
I was observing.
Which is the adult word for stalking.
And every new follower felt personal.
Not because it was.
Because my ego was bleeding.
I wasn't actually afraid he liked someone else.
I was afraid I was replaceable.
So instead of sitting with that fear like a regulated adult, I opened three apps
and tried to find proof.
Proof of what?
I'm still not entirely sure.
Proof that I mattered. Proof that he wasn't happier. Proof that I wasn't
forgettable.
And the irony?
The more I searched, the worse I felt.
Because social media is not built for emotional stability.
It is built for highlight reels.

So of course he looked fine.

People rarely post "emotionally conflicted and missing my ex."

They post tequila and good lighting.

And I interpreted tequila as closure.

That's not insight.

That's imagination.

And I had plenty of it.

"I was acting like a woman who had access to Wi-Fi and too much imagination."

And the Wi-Fi was strong.

Strong enough to keep me distracted. Strong enough to keep me busy. Strong enough to keep me from sitting still long enough to ask a harder question:

Why did I need access so badly?

Because access felt like control.

And control felt like dignity.

If I could see him, I wasn't completely erased.

Until one day, I couldn't see anything at all.

There's something uniquely humbling about realizing you've been removed.

Not slowly faded.

Removed.

One day I could see everything.

The next day, nothing.

At first, I thought it was a glitch.

Which is delusional optimism at its finest.

It was not a glitch.

I had been blocked.

And that hit differently.

Because heartbreak still leaves you access.

Blocking leaves you invisible.

And invisibility is louder than silence.

I wasn't just sad.

I was disoriented.
Rejection hurts.
Erasure stings.
But loss of control?
That's the one that made me spiral internally.
Because I didn't just lose him.
I lost the ability to monitor him.
And if I can't monitor, I can't measure.
And if I can't measure, I can't compare.
And if I can't compare...
Who am I performing for?
That's when it got uncomfortable.
Because I realized something I did not want to admit:
Part of my "moving on" was audience-based.
If he could see me thriving, I felt powerful.
If he couldn't see me at all, I felt... irrelevant.
And that's ego.
Not love.
Love grieves.
Ego tracks visibility.

Respectfully, I was grieving and tracking.
That's a dangerous combination.
But here's the twist I didn't expect:
Once I was blocked, the performance stopped.
Not immediately.
But gradually.
Because there was no longer a stage.
And when there's no stage, you either collapse...
Or you recalibrate.
That's when the real shift started.
Not when he left.
Not when I understood.

When I lost access.

Because access had been my illusion of control.
And without it, I had to sit with something raw:
Because access had been my illusion of control.
And without it, I had to sit with something raw:
I could not control how I was remembered.
I could not control what story he told himself about me.
I could not control whether I was archived, romanticized, or deleted.
I could only control how I showed up.
And for weeks, I hadn't been showing up.
I'd been monitoring.
Which is impressive considering I don't work in surveillance.

Getting blocked didn't heal me.
It humbled me.
And apparently, humility was overdue.
The humiliating part?
I genuinely believed I was above this.
I have read books. I have had therapy. I know attachment theory.
And yet.
There I was. Interpreting punctuation like a detective.
I wasn't unstable.
I was just a woman who had too much access and too many thoughts to go
with it.
Strong Wi-Fi.
Strong delusion.

I would've passed a background check. Just not an emotional one.
There was a 48-hour window where my brain suggested some truly creative
ideas.
Not violent. Just... inventive.
Like: "What if I order ten pizzas to his new place and request cash on
delivery?"

Or: "What if I casually send an Uber driver past his house just to check for unfamiliar vehicles?"

Not because I cared.

Because I was curious.

Which is the emotionally unstable cousin of caring.

And at one point, my brain said: "You still have that spare key…"

Respectfully. We will not finish that sentence.

Did I do any of it?

No.

Because I prefer dignity over felony charges.

But the fact that my brain even drafted those ideas? Humbling.

That's the kind of savage that's funny without being destructive.

And that's when I realized something slightly embarrassing:

I didn't want him back.

I wanted to win the narrative.

That's ego.

And ego will have you doing Olympic-level mental gymnastics over a man who cannot communicate consistently.

Gold medal performance. Zero prize.

Chapter 13

Modern Dating Is a Social Experiment

MODERN DATING IS NOT dating.

It's branding.

We don't meet people anymore. We assess profiles.

We don't fall in love. We analyze response time.

We don't ask, "Are we compatible?" We ask, "Are they consistent across platforms?"

I was out here cross-referencing behavior like I had a subscription to Emotional CSI.

Because modern dating doesn't just break your heart. It gives you data.

Seen at 11:42 p.m. Active 6 minutes ago. New follower. Story views. Playlist updates.

It's not romance.

It's analytics.

And I participated like I had stock in the situation.

Here's the part nobody wants to admit:

Social media turns breakups into performance reviews.

If he posts smiling, you assume he's thriving. If he posts nothing, you assume he's hiding something. If he soft-launches someone new, you zoom in like you're identifying wildlife.

And I did it too.

Fully grown woman. Paying taxes. Refreshing like I was waiting for exam results.

Modern dating doesn't reward clarity.

It rewards mystery.

It rewards detachment.

It rewards the person who cares less.

And I cared.

Which, apparently, is amateur behavior now.

We don't break up anymore.

We rebrand.

New gym routine. New aesthetic. New captions that sound suspiciously reflective.

And suddenly everyone is "at peace."

No one posts: *"Still emotionally confused and mildly spiraling."*

No.

They post sunsets.

And I interpreted sunsets as closure.

Which is wild.

Because a filtered sky is not emotional growth.

It's lighting.

And here's what I finally understood:

Modern dating makes you feel replaceable because it makes everyone look available.

There's always another profile. Another option. Another distraction.

It creates the illusion that depth is interchangeable.

It isn't.

But distraction is.

And a lot of people are very good at distraction.

The truth?

The system isn't broken.

It's designed for surface.

Quick hits. Short attention. Low investment.

And I was trying to build something long-term in a culture that rewards temporary dopamine.

That's not naïve.

It's just inconvenient.

Because when someone says, "I moved on quickly,"

What they often mean is, "I distracted myself efficiently."

That's not the same thing.

And once I saw that, something shifted.

Not bitter. Not cynical.

Just amused.

Because I wasn't crazy.

I was operating with depth in a system built for performance.

And depth doesn't trend.

It anchors.

So if modern dating feels absurd sometimes?

It's because it is.

And the only way to survive it with dignity is to stop performing inside it.

Which, unfortunately, required me to stop refreshing like I was awaiting breaking news.

Humbling.

But necessary.

CHAPTER 14

THE DAY I KNEW HE WASN'T COMING BACK

GETTING BLOCKED HUMBLED ME.

But it didn't end the waiting.

That would've been efficient.

For a while, I told myself I was fine. I had stopped checking. I had stopped performing. I had stopped drafting imaginary speeches in my head. On paper, I was healing.

In reality, I was waiting.

Not dramatically. Not publicly. Just quietly.

Like someone who says they've closed the tab but still refreshes it once a week.

I didn't call it hope. Hope sounds poetic. This wasn't poetic. It was administrative. It lived in small places. In the way my heart still jumped when my phone lit up unexpectedly. In the way I rehearsed a calm, collected, slightly mysterious version of myself — just in case he reached out.

That version of me was phenomenal.

Very composed. Very detached. Very fake.

I had prepared an entire personality for a conversation that never happened.

That's commitment.

You can be blocked and still be waiting.

You can be humbled and still leave a microscopic door unlocked.

Months passed.

Not dramatically. Just time doing its job. I rebuilt routines. I slept normally again. I stopped narrating my life for an invisible audience. But underneath all of it, there was still a quiet thread:

He'll realize.

Not today. But eventually.

Eventually is a manipulative little word.

Eventually kept me tethered.

And then one ordinary day — mid-coffee, mid-email, mid-being a functional adult — it hit me.

He isn't coming back.

Not because he's cruel. Not because I wasn't enough. Not because the universe is dramatic.

Just because he isn't.

And that realization didn't explode.

It landed.

There's a very specific grief attached to that moment. It's not chaotic. It doesn't knock you over. It settles in your chest like weight.

It's the grief of potential.

I wasn't mourning him anymore.

I was mourning the version of him I had quietly rewritten in my head.

The reflective one. The accountable one. The "I miscalculated" one.

That version never existed outside my imagination.

And admitting that was brutal.

Because it meant I wasn't waiting for him.

I was waiting for a character I had edited.

For a brief, undignified moment, I considered sending something dramatic. Not to win him back — I was past that — but to feel powerful. A perfectly phrased message. Calm. Cutting. Memorable. The kind of text that screenshots well.

I drafted it mentally.

It was excellent.

I didn't send it.

Not because I lacked courage.

Because I finally understood something I should've understood months earlier:

If someone has to rediscover your value, they never held it properly.

Clarity doesn't arrive loudly.

It arrives when you're tired of negotiating with reality.

And I was exhausted.

Exhausted from budgeting emotional space for someone who wasn't budgeting any for me.

Exhausted from pretending patience was maturity.

Exhausted from leaving the door "just in case."

So I let it end.

Not theatrically. Not angrily. Decisively.

The grief wasn't explosive.

It was cleaner than that.

It felt like deleting a future I had privately rehearsed.

I wasn't losing him in that moment.

I was losing the fantasy.

And beneath the sadness, there was relief.

Because waiting is heavier than endings.

Endings hurt once.

Waiting hurts daily.

When I stopped expecting him to circle back, something inside me loosened.

Not my standards. Not my pride. My grip.

He wasn't coming back.

And eventually—

I stopped needing him to.

Chapter 15

The Soft Launch (Narrated by National Geographic)

THERE IS A SPECIFIC phase of modern dating that deserves its own documentary.

Not a rom-com. Not a drama.

A wildlife special.

Because what we are witnessing is not subtle. It is ritual.
Observe the male in his post-breakup habitat.

Notice the re-emergence of curated selfies. The gym lighting improves. The jawline sharpens. The captions become cryptic but optimistic.

"Growth."

Fascinating.

Now observe the soft launch.

Not a hard reveal. Never a hard reveal. That would require commitment.

No, this is choreography.

A blurred hand in the corner. A cropped shoulder at dinner. A second wine glass placed just close enough to imply companionship but far enough to deny specifics.

We see you.
We all see you.
And for a brief, humbling period of time...
So did I.

I zoomed in like I was analyzing footage for a criminal investigation.
Enhance the reflection in the spoon. Is that a feminine silhouette? Pause.
Rewind. Enhance again.

Respectfully, I was unwell.

But heartbreak turns regular women into amateur detectives with Wi-Fi.
The difference between FBI and FOMO is about two letters and one ego
bruise.

And here's what's embarrassing:
I wasn't even trying to get him back.
I was trying to decode the replacement.
Is she prettier? Calmer? Less intense? Does she laugh at jokes I
overanalyzed?
And the most dangerous thought of all:
Is she easier?
There it is.
The quiet insult we throw at ourselves.
Maybe he didn't want depth. Maybe he wanted simplicity. Maybe I was a
three-season psychological drama and she's a light sitcom.

Do you see how fast the ego spirals?
I wasn't observing him.
I was ranking myself.
Olympic-level comparison. Zero medal ceremony.
And the soft launch?
It worked.

Not because it meant anything. But because it was designed to mean something.

That's the part I didn't understand at first.
The blurred shoulder isn't about love. It's about signal.
"I'm not alone." "I've moved on." "I'm thriving."

It's mating season with filters.
And for a second — just a second — it stung.
Not because I wanted him back.
But because I didn't want to be easily replaced.
There's a difference.
One is longing. The other is ego.
And ego is loud.

But here's the twist that changed everything:
If someone needs to signal so loudly that they're fine...
They probably aren't.
Secure people don't soft launch. They just live.
That realization didn't make me bitter.
It made me amused.

Because the truth is — I've soft launched too.
We all have.
Posted strategically. Timed things intentionally. Made sure a certain person would see.
We call it coincidence.
It's choreography.
And suddenly, the whole thing felt less personal.
Less tragic.
More... theatrical.

And I realized something that freed me:
If someone is performing, let them perform.

I don't buy tickets anymore.

Maybe they cared

Maybe they were just
    confused

Maybe it meant something

~~Maybe you just~~
    needed to wait

Cross out what you don't believe
anymore.

CHAPTER 16

I Thought He Was Reflecting

OR AN EMBARRASSINGLY LONG time, I assumed he was somewhere thinking deeply.

Not spiraling like I was.

But reflecting.

Processing.

Replaying conversations in his head and finally understanding my perspective.

I imagined him having quiet realizations at 1:30 a.m. The kind where you stare at the ceiling and think, "Maybe she was right."

In my mind, he was evolving.

In reality?

He might have just been... living.

That realization is humbling.

Because it forces you to admit something slightly uncomfortable:

I projected my emotional depth onto him.

I process everything.

I replay conversations. I analyze tone. I look for growth inside conflict.

So I assumed he did too.

But not everyone processes pain by dissecting it.

Some people compartmentalize. Some distract. Some detach. Some don't revisit at all.

And for a while, I mistook detachment for reflection.

I thought silence meant internal work.

It might have just meant silence.

That's where my ego got creative again.

If he wasn't reaching out, maybe he was rebuilding quietly. If he wasn't apologizing, maybe he was figuring it out. If he wasn't circling back, maybe he just needed time.

Eventually is a very flexible fantasy.

And I clung to it longer than I'd like to admit.

The funny part?

I genuinely believed he was sitting somewhere experiencing this the way I was.

Like heartbreak was a synchronized event.

As if we were both assigned the same emotional homework.

We were not.

I was journaling.

He was probably ordering food.

That's not shade.

That's realism.

Men don't necessarily attach less deeply.

But many attach differently.

Some retreat inward. Some avoid. Some shut down instead of open up.

And some simply move forward without replaying every emotional detail.

That doesn't make them monsters.

It just makes them wired differently.

The part I had to confront was this:

Just because I process through reflection doesn't mean everyone does.

And just because someone isn't revisiting the relationship internally doesn't mean they're incapable of feeling.

It might mean they're incapable of processing the way I needed them to.

That's different.

And here's the ego bruise:

I thought my emotional depth would automatically create reflection in him.

As if depth is contagious.

It's not.

Depth requires capacity.

And capacity isn't something you can project onto someone.

You either see it in action, or you imagine it.

Guess which one I was doing.

Chapter 17
We Didn't Attach the Same Way

I T TOOK ME A while to understand that we weren't grieving the same relationship, even when we were in it.

For the longest time, I assumed attachment was symmetrical. If I felt something deeply, surely he felt it too. If I replayed conversations and searched for meaning, surely he did the same. I believed emotional depth worked like gravity — if it pulled me in, it had to be pulling him too.

But attachment doesn't operate that neatly.

I attach by leaning in. When something feels uncertain, I want to talk about it. When something hurts, I want to understand it. Reflection feels productive to me. Conversation feels stabilizing. I process through connection.

He seemed to process through distance.

When things became heavy, he didn't dig in. He stepped back. Where I wanted clarity, he wanted space. Where I felt urgency, he felt overwhelm. And for a long time, I interpreted that difference as indifference.

It wasn't indifference.
It was incompatibility in processing.
That distinction matters.

Because once I stopped assuming that his silence meant he didn't care, I had to confront something more uncomfortable: he might have cared in the only way he knew how. And that way didn't align with what I needed.

Understanding attachment styles didn't excuse anything. It didn't rewrite behavior. It didn't make the ending softer. What it did was remove the personalization.

He didn't detach to punish me.
He detached because that's how he regulates.
I pursued clarity because that's how I regulate.
And when one person regulates through closeness and the other regulates through withdrawal, conflict becomes inevitable.

For a long time, I framed that as imbalance. As though one of us was more evolved. The truth is less dramatic than that. We were wired differently, and neither of us had the tools to bridge that gap.

The part I had to own was this: I kept expecting him to respond to emotional intensity the way I would. I assumed that if something mattered to me, it would eventually matter to him in the same tone, at the same volume.

But attachment isn't contagious.

You can't love someone into matching your emotional depth. You can't explain someone into feeling safe enough to stay present. And you certainly can't argue someone into regulating the way you do.

Once I understood that, the story shifted.

It stopped being about who cared more.
It became about who could sustain the kind of connection I wanted.
That realization didn't make me superior.

It made me realistic.
And realism is quieter than blame.

this is where it changed.

CHAPTER 18

I Was Unbothered. Loudly.

THERE WAS A VERY specific phase where I claimed I was unbothered.

Out loud.

Frequently.

Unprompted.

Which, historically, is not how genuinely unbothered people behave.

I said things like, "It's fine."

It was not fine.

I said, "I don't care."

I cared aggressively.

I once told a friend, "Honestly, I'm good."

Then immediately checked his story viewers to see if he had watched mine.

Unbothered.

Loudly.

The performance was impressive.

I mastered the art of looking emotionally stable while internally running a full investigative task force.

He would take four hours to respond, and I would respond twelve minutes later to maintain composure optics.

Not too fast. Not too slow. Strategically stable.

Nothing screams security like calculated response timing.

I told myself I was protecting my dignity.

In reality, I was protecting my ego.

Because admitting I was bothered felt weak.

So instead, I acted detached.

Detached people don't draft responses and then delete them three times.

Detached people don't stare at "typing…" bubbles like they're awaiting a verdict.

Detached people do not rehearse indifference in the mirror.

I did.

With conviction.

And let's talk about the romanticizing of crumbs during this phase.

He sent one thoughtful message.

One.

And I mentally restored his character arc.

"He's growing."

From what? A single paragraph?

The bar wasn't low.

The bar was negotiable.

And I negotiated enthusiastically.

I mistook small improvements for transformation.

Because if he was transforming, then my patience had meaning.

I wasn't waiting. I was investing.

Which sounds mature.

It was not.

It was hope wearing a business suit.

And I was impressed with it.

There's something deeply humbling about realizing you were performing indifference while begging internally for reassurance.

I wanted him to see that I was fine.

Thriving. Glowing. Unshakeable.

Meanwhile, I was refreshing apps like it was cardio.

I wasn't crazy.

I was uncomfortable.

And instead of admitting that, I curated.

I curated posts. I curated timing. I curated tone.

I didn't block him. I curated for him.

Which is significantly more exhausting.

The funniest part?

The moment I actually stopped caring...

I stopped performing.

There was no announcement.

No cryptic quote. No strategic silence.

Just absence.

Real unbothered is quiet.

It doesn't need witnesses.

And that's how I knew something had shifted.

Because when I was finally okay...

I forgot to prove it.

CHAPTER 19

THE ERA OF OVERCORRECTION

G ETTING BLOCKED SHOULD HAVE ended the performance.

It didn't.

If anything, it intensified it.

Because when someone removes access, your ego doesn't surrender.

It strategizes.

He blocked me.

Who's to say the algorithm wouldn't carry my glow-up across digital borders?

Who's to say a mutual wouldn't "accidentally" mention how well I was doing?

Who's to say he wasn't watching from a shadow account like an emotionally unavailable Batman?

Ridiculous.

And yet, completely believable at the time.

Because blocking doesn't kill ego.

It activates strategy.

That's how the overcorrection era began.

There was a brief and deeply unnecessary phase where I decided the solution to heartbreak was performance.

Not emotional growth.

Performance.

If he could move on efficiently, then I could move on theatrically.

Suddenly I was "so busy." So unbothered. So mysteriously unavailable.

I did not cry.

I curated.

There is something incredibly humbling about realizing you're posting stories you hope someone specific will see... while claiming you're not performing.

I was not subtle.

If I went out, I documented it. If I laughed, I made sure it was visible. If I looked good, I uploaded proof.

This was not healing.

This was marketing.

And I was my own PR team.

I convinced myself I was detached.

But detachment doesn't check who viewed your story.

Detachment doesn't wonder if that photo looked like you were "doing better."

Detachment doesn't wear red lipstick out of spite.

And I absolutely wore red lipstick out of spite.

Not because I like red lipstick.

Because red lipstick feels like emotional revenge.

I wasn't angry.

I was strategic.

Which is worse.

At one point I told a friend, very calmly, "I genuinely don't care anymore."

And then refreshed three apps in under a minute.

Olympic-level contradiction.

I wasn't trying to get him back.

I was trying to win the breakup.

Which is not a real competition.

But tell that to my nervous system.

This is the part no one posts about.

The overcorrection era.

Where you swing so hard into "I'm thriving" that you look like you're campaigning.

I was suddenly hyper-independent.

Booked things I didn't even want to do.

Said yes to events I was too tired for.

Laughed louder than necessary.

Because nothing says emotional stability like forced enthusiasm.

And the entire time, I told myself:

"This is growth."

It was not growth.

It was ego in athleisure.

Modern dating has turned moving on into an aesthetic.

You don't just heal.

You rebrand.

New playlist. New captions. New gym routine. New angle of your face.

And I participated.

Full adult. Full awareness. Full Wi-Fi.

It's wild how quickly "self-improvement" becomes "prove you're fine."

And I was determined to prove.

Not to him.

To myself.

Which is somehow more embarrassing.

The funniest part?

Underneath all of it, I was still anxious.

Not about losing him.

About being forgettable.

Which are two different fears.

Anxiety doesn't disappear just because you post better photos.

It just wears better outfits.

And I mistook that adrenaline for empowerment.

That wasn't empowerment.

That was cortisol in good lighting.

Eventually, something felt off.

Not morally.

Emotionally.

Because pretending not to care requires constant energy.

And I was tired.

Tired of performing unbothered.

Tired of rehearsing indifference.

Tired of trying to look healed instead of actually being it.

Overcorrection is exhausting.

Because it's still orbiting the same person.

Just from a different angle.

And that's when I had to admit something slightly uncomfortable:

If I'm still performing, I'm still attached.

Not to him.

To the narrative.

To the idea that I needed to "win."

And winning what?

A man who couldn't communicate consistently?

Let's be serious.

There's nothing iconic about overcorrection.

It's just ego with better lighting.

And once I saw that clearly, the energy shifted.

Not dramatically.

Not in a self-help montage way.

Just quietly.

I stopped posting for invisible viewers.

I stopped dressing for emotional warfare.

I stopped pretending I was unbothered.

Because real unbothered doesn't announce itself.

It just lives.

And for the first time, I wasn't trying to look okay.

I was trying to be okay.

Much less glamorous.

Much more effective.

CHAPTER 20

The Girl Who Thought She Was Replaceable

THERE WAS A VERSION of me who genuinely believed I was interchangeable. Not in a dramatic, cinematic way. In a logistical one. Like if I stepped out of the frame, someone else could slide in and the storyline would continue with minimal disruption. I didn't say that out loud, obviously. Out loud, I was confident. Internally, I was calculating.

I adjusted myself like I was competing in a silent contest no one officially announced. I tried to be agreeable but not boring. Interesting but not intimidating. Emotional but not "too much." **I curated my personality like it was a limited edition release.** As if my value increased the less maintenance I required.

That's not confidence.

That's strategy.

And strategy is usually a sign you don't feel secure in your position.

The truth is, once I started noticing how easily he seemed to move through people, I internalized it. Not consciously. But subtly. If connection looked replaceable to him, maybe I was. So instead of holding my ground, I optimized. I became easier. More understanding. More flexible. I framed it as maturity.

It wasn't maturity.

It was fear.

Fear that if I didn't make myself low-friction, I'd be swapped out.

Which is wild when you think about it. Because I was the one showing up consistently. I was the one communicating. I was the one trying to build something stable. And yet somehow I was the one acting like I needed to prove I was worth keeping.

That's embarrassing.

But it's honest.

Social media doesn't help. When someone reappears next to someone new, it creates the illusion that connection is modular — like anyone can be inserted into the same aesthetic and the storyline continues. And if you're not careful, you start competing with a highlight reel that was never real to begin with. I told myself I wasn't competing.

I absolutely was.

Not directly. Not aggressively. But internally, I was measuring. Are they calmer? Prettier? More agreeable? Less intense? Did he seem lighter because I was heavy? These were not elegant thoughts. They were survival thoughts disguised as analysis.

And the worst part? I didn't even want to be chosen by someone who required me to shrink. But I still wanted to win.

That's ego.

Not love.

Love doesn't require optimization.

Ego does.

Looking back, I can see how much of my energy went toward being impressive instead of being grounded. I wanted to be unforgettable. But I was operating from the fear that I wasn't. That if I didn't constantly offer value, depth, flexibility, humor, patience — I'd be replaced.

Which is exhausting.

And slightly insulting to myself.

Because I am not a position that needs to be defended. I am not a slot that can be filled. I am not interchangeable inventory in someone's emotional warehouse.

But I acted like I was.

And that's the part I had to confront.

It wasn't that I was replaceable.

It was that I believed I might be.

There's a difference.

One is a fact.

The other is a story.

And I had been operating from the story.

Once I saw that clearly, something shifted. Not dramatically. Not in a self-help revelation kind of way. Just enough to make me pause the next time I felt the urge to adjust myself for someone else's comfort.

Because if someone experiences connection as disposable, that doesn't make me disposable.

It just makes us incompatible.

And incompatibility is not a character flaw.

It's a filter.

I don't need to be irreplaceable to everyone.

I need to be aligned with someone who doesn't treat connection like it's interchangeable.

That's different.

And it's quieter.

And it's much less chaotic.

CHAPTER 21

I Mistook Anxiety for Chemistry

THERE IS A VERY uncomfortable realization that happens when you replay a relationship honestly: what I called "chemistry" was often just anxiety with good lighting. It felt electric. It felt intense. It felt meaningful. My stomach flipped. My thoughts raced. I analyzed everything. I cared deeply and immediately. I thought that meant it was powerful.

It wasn't powerful.

It was activating.

And activation feels like connection when you don't know the difference.

I thought the unpredictability was depth. I thought the emotional distance meant he was complex. I told myself, "He's just guarded." Guarded sounded romantic. It sounded like there was something to unlock. And apparently I appointed myself the locksmith.

There's something seductive about being the one who gets let in. It feels special. It feels earned. It feels intimate. But earning emotional access is not the same thing as building emotional safety. And I confused those two repeatedly.

When he pulled away, I leaned in. When he became vague, I became more expressive. When he hesitated, I doubled my effort. I framed it as commitment. In reality, it was my nervous system trying to stabilize something unstable.

Anxiety creates urgency. Urgency creates attachment. Attachment masquerades as chemistry.

That cycle is intoxicating.

Because when he was warm, it felt euphoric. When he was distant, it felt devastating. And that contrast? That rollercoaster? I interpreted it as passion. But passion that depends on inconsistency is not passion. It's volatility.

Calm never gave me butterflies.

And I mistook that for boredom.

Which is tragic, in hindsight.

I didn't crave chaos. I craved certainty. But I kept choosing people who felt exciting because they were unclear. There's a difference between mystery and misalignment. Mystery invites curiosity. Misalignment invites anxiety. I kept calling misalignment "interesting."

That's on me.

Modern dating glorifies that feeling. The push-pull. The slow replies. The ambiguity. It frames anxiety as attraction. If you're not slightly nervous, are you even interested? If you're not analyzing, are you even invested?

I bought into that narrative.

Fully.

The problem is, anxiety bonds you to potential, not reality. You don't fall in love with who someone is. You fall in love with the relief you feel when they temporarily choose you. That's not intimacy. That's intermittent reinforcement.

And intermittent reinforcement is addictive.

Once I understood that, I had to admit something slightly humiliating: I wasn't addicted to him. I was addicted to the cycle. The reassurance. The spike. The relief.

It's hard to call something chemistry when you realize it was cortisol.

But that's the truth.

And the truth is quieter than the fantasy.

Healthy connection doesn't require decoding. It doesn't require performing. It doesn't require guessing. It doesn't require earning.

It requires alignment.
And alignment feels calm.
I used to think calm meant boring.
Now I understand it means safe.
That shift changed everything.

He didn't text.

That was the answer.

you already knew.
you just didn't stop.

CHAPTER 22

WHY CONFUSION FELT LIKE DEPTH

THERE WAS A TIME when I genuinely believed confusion meant something meaningful was happening.

If I felt slightly off-balance, I assumed it was intensity. If I couldn't quite read him, I told myself it was complexity. If I left a conversation unsure where I stood, I called it mystery.

It never occurred to me that clarity might simply feel calm.

And calm, at the time, felt suspiciously boring.

I remember one night specifically. Nothing dramatic happened. That's the point. We were texting. The conversation was warm, then cool, then warm again. He'd say something that made me feel close, then follow it with something distant. Not cruel. Just slightly off. Slightly vague. Slightly non-committal.

And instead of asking directly what that meant, I analyzed it.

For hours.

I reread messages like they were coded language. I tried to determine if the warmth was genuine or temporary. I asked myself if I had imagined the shift. I adjusted my tone accordingly. Softer here. Less intense there. Maybe I had miscalculated.

That mental gymnastics routine became normal.

And I mistook the effort for depth.

Because if something takes work to decode, it must be layered. Right?

Wrong.

Sometimes it's just unclear.

There's a difference between depth and confusion. Depth invites you in. Confusion keeps you guessing. Depth feels like discovery. Confusion feels like instability.

But instability can feel intoxicating when you're emotionally invested.

I would leave interactions feeling slightly unsettled and call it "processing." I'd tell myself, "He just thinks differently." Or, "He's guarded." Or my personal favorite: "He's not used to someone like me."

Which sounds empowering.

But was actually ego trying to make sense of inconsistency.

There's something addictive about trying to be the exception. The one who finally understands him. The one who breaks through the walls. It makes you feel chosen in advance, even when you're not chosen in reality.

And the more unclear things felt, the more I leaned in.

That's the part I had to confront.

Clarity would have felt secure.

But secure didn't trigger adrenaline.

Confusion did.

I once dated someone who was very direct. He communicated clearly. He didn't leave me guessing. If he liked me, he said it. If he was busy, he said that too. No guessing games. No strategic silences. No emotional riddles.

And I remember thinking, "This feels... flat."

Flat.

Because my nervous system wasn't activated.

It was calm.

And calm, at that stage in my life, felt like something was missing.

Nothing was missing.

I just wasn't used to safety.

That realization hit harder than any breakup.

Because it meant the pattern wasn't random.

It was familiar.

But intensity without stability is just noise.

Depth doesn't require decoding.

It doesn't require adjusting yourself to keep someone engaged.

It doesn't require strategic restraint.

It just exists.

And if I'm honest, part of me didn't fully trust that kind of simplicity. Because if it's simple, there's nothing to chase. Nothing to prove. Nothing to unlock.

And chasing had become my identity.

When I stopped romanticizing confusion, I had to admit something uncomfortable: some of what I labeled "complex men" were just inconsistent men.

That's not poetic. But it's honest.

And honesty is far less dramatic than fantasy.

CHAPTER 23

I Wasn't Attracted to Him. I Was Attracted to the Challenge.

FOR A LONG TIME, I thought I was drawn to depth.

Intelligence. Mystery. Emotional complexity.

That sounds refined.

It sounds evolved.

It sounds like something you say while holding a glass of wine and pretending you've always had standards.

But if I'm honest, what I was actually drawn to was resistance.

I liked the slight distance. The subtle withdrawal. The feeling that I had to lean in just a little more to be fully chosen.

I told myself it meant he was careful.

Measured.

Guarded.

What it really meant was he wasn't fully available.

And for reasons I didn't examine at the time, that felt compelling.

There's something intoxicating about almost.

Almost understood. Almost secure. Almost prioritized.

It keeps you engaged.

It keeps you trying.

It keeps you proving.

And I was very good at proving.

I could be patient. Supportive. Low-maintenance. Understanding.

I could translate silence into "he just needs space."

I could reinterpret inconsistency as "he's overwhelmed."

I could spin emotional absence into something poetic.

Which is impressive.

And mildly delusional.

I didn't fall for him.

I fell for the idea that if I could get him to open fully, it would mean I was special.

That I was different.

That I had unlocked something other women hadn't.

That's not love.

That's competition disguised as devotion.

And it's embarrassingly relatable.

Because nothing makes you feel powerful like being chosen by someone who doesn't choose easily.

The ego loves exclusivity.

Even when exclusivity comes with emotional drought.

Stable attention felt predictable.

Predictable felt boring.

Boring felt unsafe.

That part took me longer to admit.

Because somewhere along the line, I confused adrenaline with compatibility.

If I had to wonder where I stood, I felt engaged.

If I felt calm, I felt suspicious.

Peace didn't feel like connection.

It felt like something was missing.

And that says more about my nervous system than it does about any man.

I wasn't chasing chaos.

I was chasing activation.

That tight feeling in your chest. That mental replay. That constant analysis.

I mistook that intensity for chemistry.

But chemistry doesn't require confusion.

And attraction doesn't require instability.

The challenge was never him.

The challenge was me trying to earn certainty from someone who couldn't provide it consistently.

And I took that personally.

Which, in hindsight, was unnecessary.

Here's the uncomfortable realization:

I was attracted to people who felt slightly out of reach.

Not because I lacked worth.

Because I liked proving I could bridge the distance.

If he was steady, there was nothing to win.

If he was distant, there was a mission.

And I do love a mission.

Even when it costs me sleep.

When I say I've grown, this is what I mean.

Not that I no longer feel attracted.

Not that I no longer care.

But I no longer romanticize emotional unavailability as depth.

If I have to decode you, convince you, stabilize you, or unlock you, that's not chemistry.

That's labor.

And I am retired.

Not bitter.

Not dramatic.

Just observant.

The truth is simple and slightly humbling:

I wasn't addicted to him.

I was addicted to the feeling of earning love.

And once I stopped finding that impressive, everything changed.

Now, when something feels confusing, I don't lean in.
I lean back.
Not to play a game.
But to see if there's actually something solid there.
If there is, it remains.
If there isn't, it fades.
And I no longer interpret fading as failure.
Sometimes it's just clarity arriving on time.
That's the difference now.
I don't chase distance.
I don't compete for attention.
And I don't mistake emotional resistance for mystery.
I'm not looking for someone to unlock.
I'm looking for someone already open.
Which is significantly less dramatic.
And significantly more peaceful.
And surprisingly attractive.

Chapter 24

My Standards Didn't Get Higher, They Got Clearer

OR A WHILE, I thought "raising my standards" meant becoming intimidating.

Mysterious. Harder to access. Less expressive. Emotionally bulletproof.

Which is hilarious, because nothing says healed like pretending you don't have feelings.

What I eventually realized is that my standards didn't need to become taller.

They needed to become simpler.

I didn't need grand gestures. I didn't need constant reassurance. I didn't need a perfectly curated romance.

I needed consistency.

Which, apparently, is radical.

I used to think intensity meant effort.

Now I understand effort is boring.

Effort looks like: Calling when you say you will. Replying without strategy. Following through without drama.

No fireworks. No cliffhangers. No emotional scavenger hunts.

Just steady presence.

And I used to find that underwhelming.

Because chaos had trained my nervous system to expect plot twists.

Stability felt quiet. And quiet felt suspicious.

So when something didn't make me anxious, I assumed it wasn't deep.

Which is both self-aware and deeply embarrassing.

Upgrading my standards wasn't glamorous.

It was uncomfortable.

It meant walking away earlier. It meant not explaining myself twelve different ways. It meant not translating emotional laziness into "he's just processing."

I stopped auditioning. Not because I became detached. Because I became uninterested in convincing.

That's different.

I no longer need to win someone over.

If they're unsure, I am not the solution.

And that sentence would have terrified an earlier version of me.

There's something quietly powerful about not needing to be chosen dramatically.

I don't need the chase. I don't need the redemption arc. I don't need someone to realize I was "the one" months later.

If you see it, you see it.

If you don't, I don't audition.

And this time I mean it.

Upgraded standards don't scream.

They don't post about being unbothered. They don't deliver speeches.

They simply remove access.

Calmly. Without announcement.

And the most surprising part?

Peace is not boring.

It's just unfamiliar when you've been conditioned to confuse adrenaline with connection.

Now when something feels confusing, I don't investigate.

I observe.

And if it doesn't feel grounded, I disengage.

Not angrily.
Not theatrically.
Just clearly.
That's the difference now.

They were busy ___________________

They needed space _________________

They were overwhelmed _________

They _________________________________

Fill in the rest yourself.

CHAPTER 25
THE FIRST TIME I DIDN'T REACT

T WASN'T DRAMATIC.

There was no cinematic clarity, no background music, no inner monologue announcing transformation. It was smaller than that. Almost boring.

His name popped up somewhere — not even a message. A tagged photo. A casual reference. Something that, six months earlier, would have sent me into a quiet spiral disguised as "just checking."

And I didn't flinch.

That's how subtle it was.

No tightening in my chest. No immediate comparison. No urge to decode tone or posture or background details like I was preparing a court case.

I just... noticed it.

And kept moving.

The strangest part wasn't that I didn't react. It was that I didn't have to suppress the reaction. It simply wasn't there.

That's when I realized something slightly uncomfortable.

For months, I had believed I was healing because I understood the psychology. I could name attachment styles. I could explain ego wounds. I could dissect the difference between confusion and depth with academic precision.

But none of that meant I was free.
Freedom wasn't insight.
Freedom was indifference.
Not coldness. Not bitterness. Not pretending.
Just the absence of activation.
That was new.

I had spent so much time trying to win the narrative, win the emotional high ground, win the invisible comparison battle, that I forgot the actual goal was peace.
And peace is quiet.
It doesn't post. It doesn't signal. It doesn't soft launch itself.
It just stops caring.
I didn't feel superior. I didn't feel evolved. I didn't feel victorious.
I felt neutral.

And for someone who once interpreted punctuation like a personality trait, neutrality felt elite.
That was the first moment I knew the upgrade was real.
Not because I raised my standards. Because I no longer needed to measure myself against someone who couldn't meet them.

That shift wasn't loud.
It was internal.
And internal shifts are the only ones that stick.

Chapter 26
How I Date Now

T HERE WAS A TIME when I mistook intensity for intimacy. I thought if something felt electric, it must be meaningful. If someone confused me, it meant there was depth. If I felt slightly anxious, it meant I cared.

Now I know better.
Now, if I feel anxious in the beginning, I don't romanticize it. I investigate it.
Not him.
Me.
Because calm has become more attractive to me than chemistry ever was.

And that shift didn't happen loudly. It happened quietly, after I got tired of decoding grown men like they were encrypted files.
I don't read into punctuation anymore. I read into patterns.
If someone is inconsistent, I don't assume they're complex. I assume they're inconsistent.
If someone sends mixed signals, I don't lean in harder. I lean back.
And if I have to ask myself three times whether something feels right, it usually doesn't.

I no longer audition.
Not dramatically. Not with speeches. I just stop over-performing.

I don't shrink my tone. I don't soften my needs. I don't pretend confusion is passion.

If a man likes me, I let him like me.

If he's unsure, I let him be unsure — somewhere else.

The biggest change isn't that I became colder.

It's that I became calmer.

There's a difference.

Cold is defensive. Calm is certain.

I used to think strength meant proving I wasn't affected. Now I know strength is being honest about what I want and refusing to negotiate it down to stay chosen.

Modern dating is chaotic. Everyone is curated. Everyone is filtering. Everyone is performing something.

But I don't feel the urge to compete anymore.

If someone wants depth, I have it.

If someone wants convenience, I'm not it.

And that used to scare me.

Now it filters for me.

I don't chase clarity anymore.

I observe.

If it's confusing, it's a no. If it's rushed, it's a no. If it feels like I'm working harder than the other person, it's a no.

Not bitter. Not dramatic. Just efficient.

Because peace is more attractive to me than potential.

And here's the part that surprised me most:

I don't feel injured anymore.

I feel amused.

Amused that I once thought unpredictability was romantic. Amused that I once mistook adrenaline for love. Amused that I once believed if I explained myself better, someone would finally understand.

The right person does not require a presentation.
He requires presence.
And I finally have that for myself.

it stopped feeling personal.

CHAPTER 27

I Leveled Up — Quietly

I DIDN'T BECOME SOFTER. I became clearer.

And clarity doesn't need a soundtrack. It doesn't need a caption. It doesn't need a "watch this" energy.

It just changes how you move.

After everything — the spirals, the ego bruises, the late-night Wi-Fi investigations like I was solving a federal case instead of nursing a breakup — something settled.

Not my heart.

My standards.

And for the first time, I stopped negotiating them like they were a limited-time offer.

Not aggressively. Not bitterly. Just... efficiently.

There's a difference between becoming cold and becoming unavailable for nonsense. I didn't ice over. I just stopped explaining basic emotional literacy to grown men like it was a community service project.

Modern dating is wild.

Everyone says they want connection. Nobody wants discomfort. Everyone says they want honesty. Nobody wants to feel exposed by it. Everyone says they want depth — until depth requires accountability.

And somehow we're all pretending that confusion is chemistry and mixed signals are intrigue.

They're not.

They're scheduling issues with a personality.

Social media didn't help. Now you're not just dating a person. You're dating their options. Their algorithm. Their curated persona. Their highlight reel. Their backup conversations.

You're competing with people who don't even exist in real life — just filtered versions of them.

And I used to play that game.

I used to think I needed to be more interesting. Less intense. More mysterious. Less available. More "chill." Less real.

Which is hilarious, because nothing says "healthy connection" like strategically muting your personality.

Exhausting.

The level up wasn't becoming harder to get.

It was becoming harder to access.

That's different.

I stopped auditioning.

I stopped performing calm when I felt confused. I stopped pretending I didn't care when I did. I stopped shrinking my expectations to make someone else feel taller.

And here's what shocked me:

When you stop auditioning, the room changes.

Some people leave.

Good.

Some people get uncomfortable.

Better.

Some people step up.

Interesting.

I don't chase. I don't overexplain. I don't rebrand myself to fit someone's comfort zone.

If someone feels confused about me, I don't clarify my existence.

Clarity is available.

Performance is retired.

And that shift didn't feel like revenge.

It felt like relief.

Not dramatic relief.

Not "I'm healed and glowing and above it all" relief.

Adult relief.

The kind where you look back at your old self and think:

You weren't crazy.

You were trying too hard for someone who wasn't trying at all.

Respectfully...

Never again.

CHAPTER 28

THE ALGORITHM IS NOT YOUR SOULMATE

THERE WAS A MOMENT — a very specific, humbling moment — where I realized I wasn't jealous of a person.

I was jealous of a filter.

And that is not something I'm proud to admit.

I saw a photo.

Perfect lighting. Perfect skin. Perfect proportions. Perfect everything.

And for a split second, my brain went:

"Oh. So that's the upgrade."

Except it wasn't a person.

It was an edited version of one.

And here's the uncomfortable truth:

We are not competing with reality anymore. We are competing with curated illusions.

Modern dating isn't just about chemistry.

It's about presentation.

You're not just meeting someone. You're meeting their highlight reel.

And somewhere along the way, we all agreed to pretend that filtered perfection is normal.

We blur. We smooth. We enhance. We contour digitally.

We become avatars.
And then we wonder why real-life connection feels underwhelming.

Because real life has pores.
Real life has angles.
Real life has bad lighting and human expressions that don't pause for retakes.

And I realized something important:
I wasn't insecure about her.
I was insecure about the illusion.
That's different.
The algorithm rewards fantasy.
But relationships require reality.
And those two don't coexist comfortably.

At some point, I had to ask myself a brutal question:
Why am I trying to compete in a digital beauty contest for someone who couldn't even show up emotionally?
Respectfully — that math is embarrassing.
If a man can be distracted by a heavily filtered illusion but overwhelmed by emotional depth, that's not a competition.
That's clarity.

And here's where it gets savage:
The more I stopped trying to look impressive online, the more grounded I felt offline.
I don't need to look like a CGI character.
I need to look like myself.
If someone prefers fantasy, they can date fantasy.
I'm not airbrushing my personality to win a temporary audience.

And here's the plot twist:
The moment you stop competing, you become rare.

Because authenticity is not algorithm-friendly.

But it is relationship-friendly.

And I'd rather be chosen in reality than admired in pixels.

<del>they cared</del>

<del>they lied</del>

<del>they lied</del>

<del>it was love</del>

<del>it was convenient</del>

<del>i mattered</del>

<del>i was used</del>

the truth hurts.

CHAPTER 29

EMOTIONALLY UNAVAILABLE BUT CHRONICALLY ONLINE

THERE'S A VERY SPECIFIC type of modern man I had to learn not to take personally.

The one who says he's "not ready for anything serious" but is very ready for daily Instagram activity.

He's overwhelmed by commitment but somehow has the emotional bandwidth to like 47 bikini photos before breakfast.

Fascinating.

He doesn't "do labels."

But he does do Snapchat streaks.

He wants something "natural."

Which usually means: no pressure, no accountability, no structure, no clarity — but consistent access to you.

Minimal responsibility. Maximum availability.

That's not confusion.

That's convenience.

And listen — I'm not anti-men.

I'm anti-ambiguity disguised as depth.

If you say you're emotionally unavailable, I believe you.

I just don't translate that into "challenge accepted" anymore.

Because somewhere in my early healing era, I thought:
Maybe he just hasn't met the right emotional environment.

Ma'am.
You are not a rehabilitation center.
You are a human being.
There's also the modern paradox:
Men who say they want "soft, feminine energy" but bring the emotional stability of a Wi-Fi signal in a basement.

You want calm?
Be steady.
You want nurturing?
Be safe.
You want loyalty?
Lead with clarity.

It's wild how many people want princess treatment without prince responsibility.
And I used to take that personally.
I used to think if I communicated better, softer, differently, strategically —maybe he would feel secure enough to show up.

But here's what I've learned:
Emotionally unavailable people don't need persuasion.
They need awareness.
And awareness is not my side quest.

If someone can scroll for hours but can't sit in a five-minute uncomfortable conversation?
That's not depth avoidance.
That's emotional laziness with good lighting.
And the funniest part?
The more I stopped trying to decode it, the clearer it became.

If a man is confused about you, he's not confused.
He's undecided.

And I am no longer auditioning for a role that requires me to shrink, guess, perform, or compete with pixels.
If you want something casual, say that.
If you want something real, act like it.
If you want both, that's not complexity.
That's contradiction.
And I don't negotiate with contradictions anymore.
Not loudly.
Just efficiently.

CHAPTER 30

STANDARDS WITHOUT SERMONS

SOMEWHERE BETWEEN SPIRALING AND leveling up, I realized something slightly inconvenient:

Standards are easy to talk about.

They're harder to apply.

It's very simple to post, "Know your worth."

It's much less simple to walk away when someone shows you they don't.

Because standards don't feel empowering in the moment.

They feel inconvenient.

They require you to leave situations that still have potential.

And potential is addictive.

For a long time, I thought having standards meant being rigid.

Demanding. Cold. Unapproachable.

In reality, it just meant being observant.

Not hypervigilant. Not suspicious. Just observant.

There's a difference between someone having a bad day and someone having a pattern.

And I used to confuse the two.

I'd excuse behavior because "everyone's human."

Which is true.

But repeated inconsistency is not humanity.

It's information.

That shift changed everything.

Because instead of asking, *"How do I fix this?"* I started asking, *"Is this something I want to live with?"*

That question is terrifying.

Because sometimes the answer is no.

And no requires action.

Standards without sermons means I don't need to announce them.

I don't need to educate anyone into understanding them.

I don't need to argue my boundaries like a thesis defense.

I just act accordingly.

If someone disappears for three days without explanation, I don't spiral.

I observe.

If someone communicates clearly and consistently, I lean in.

If someone is vague, evasive, or performative, I lean out.

It's not dramatic.

It's efficient.

And here's the funny part:

The less I explained my standards, the more peaceful I felt.

Because I stopped trying to convince people to rise to them.

I let behavior speak.

And behavior is very articulate.

Modern dating culture tries to convince you that you're asking for too much.

Consistency is "pressure."

Clarity is "intense."

Directness is "aggressive."

No.

Clarity just filters out people who prefer confusion.

And confusion benefits the person who doesn't want to commit.

Not the one who wants stability.

I don't need to announce that I value effort.

If someone values me, it will show.

If they don't, that will also show.

The difference now is I don't negotiate with the evidence.

That's the level up.

Not becoming colder.

Becoming clearer.

Not becoming unavailable.

Becoming selective.

Not becoming demanding.

Becoming done explaining why basic respect matters.

Standards don't have to be loud.

They just have to be consistent.

And I finally became consistent with myself.

CHAPTER 31

If It's Confusing, It's A No

THERE WAS A TIME when I believed confusion meant complexity.

If something felt unclear, I assumed there must be depth behind it. Maybe he was guarded. Maybe he had past trauma. Maybe he just needed patience.

Maybe I just needed to decode better.

I treated mixed signals like emotional Sudoku.

If he pulled back, I leaned in thoughtfully. If he disappeared, I gave space strategically. If he came back warm, I interpreted it as progress.

I was not confused.

I was invested.

There's a difference.

But here's what no one tells you: confusion is rarely mysterious.

It's usually clarity in disguise.

If someone likes you, you can feel it.

If someone values you, you can see it.

If someone is unsure about you, you will absolutely feel that too.

And I used to think "unsure" was something I could influence.

As if emotional consistency were unlocked by correct behavior.

Like there was a combination code:

Respond calmly. Don't overreact. Be warm but not clingy. Be soft but not needy. Be available but not too available.

Ma'am.

That's not romance.

That's project management.

Modern dating has turned ambiguity into a personality trait.

Being hard to read is now considered interesting.

Delayed responses are mysterious.

Vague intentions are "going with the flow."

No.

If I need a decoder ring to understand where I stand, that's not depth.

That's avoidance.

And avoidance does not require my empathy.

It requires distance.

There's something deeply freeing about realizing you don't have to solve people.

You don't have to interpret energy shifts like they're stock market trends.

You don't have to wait for clarity to eventually arrive.

You can decide.

And that's the shift.

I stopped asking, "What does he mean?"

And started asking, "How does this feel?"

If I feel steady, I stay.

If I feel confused, I step back.

If I feel like I'm slowly negotiating my peace to understand someone's inconsistency, I leave.

Not dramatically.

Not loudly.

Just decisively.

Because here's the uncomfortable truth:

Confusion benefits the person who isn't ready.

It rarely benefits the person who cares.

And I care too much about my own sanity now to sit in gray areas that never turn solid.

If it's confusing, it's a no.
Not because I'm rigid.
Because I'm calm.
Not because I'm bitter.
Because I'm tired of translating behavior into hope.
Clarity feels peaceful.
Confusion feels anxious.

And I finally learned to trust the difference.

CHAPTER 32
CALM IS A POWER MOVE

THERE WAS A VERSION of me that needed reactions.

Closure conversations. Final explanations. Emotional clarity wrapped in neat sentences.

Now?

I don't need theatrics.

I need peace.

And peace is not loud.

It doesn't subtweet. It doesn't announce growth. It doesn't post inspirational captions at 2 a.m.

It just... moves differently.

The most surprising part of leveling up wasn't becoming colder.

It was becoming slower to react.

Someone pulls back? I don't chase. Someone is inconsistent? I don't negotiate. Someone misunderstands me? I don't perform a clarification tour.

I used to think calm meant I didn't care.

Now I know calm means I don't panic.

And that's powerful.

Because panic is what kept me explaining myself in rooms that were already undecided.

Calm doesn't beg.
Calm observes.
Calm lets people show who they are without interrupting the demonstration.

And here's the wild part:
When you stop reacting, people get uncomfortable.
Not because you're mean.
Because you're no longer predictable.
There's nothing dramatic about my boundaries now.
They're boring.
Consistent.
Unemotional.
Which is way more unsettling than rage.
I don't need to prove I've healed.
I don't need to prove I've grown.
I don't even need to prove I'm unbothered.
Because I am.
And the quiet shift from chaos to calibration?
That's the real power move.

CHAPTER 33

I Retired That Personality

I F YOU MET ME now, you wouldn't recognize the girl who zoomed into Instagram stories like she was analyzing security footage.

I wouldn't recognize her either.

She was committed.

Deeply.

To the investigation.

I really thought emotional confusion was a puzzle to solve.

Like if I just cared correctly enough, decoded correctly enough, softened correctly enough—

it would stabilize.

Adorable.

I used to think growth would feel dramatic.

It doesn't.

It feels slightly embarrassing in hindsight.

Because once you see clearly, you can't unsee it.

And I see it now.

The delayed replies. The strategic distance. The filtered fantasy competition. The "I'm not ready but I still want access." The audition energy. The overcorrection phase.

I really went through all of it.

Like a full syllabus.

And I passed.

Barely.

Here's the real level up:

I don't panic anymore.

If something feels off, I don't convince myself it's depth. If someone is inconsistent, I don't rebrand it as "complex. "If I feel anxious, I don't romanticize it.

I identify it.

And I move.

Calmly.

That's the part that surprises me.

I didn't become harder.

I became harder to destabilize.

There's a difference.

I don't need to be chosen.

I don't need to be decoded.

I don't need to be filtered into someone's ideal.

And I definitely don't need to compete with pixels.

If it's confusing, it's a no. If it's inconsistent, it's information. If it requires me shrinking, performing, negotiating, explaining, or proving—

respectfully... never again.

And the funniest part?

I'm not even angry.

I'm slightly amused.

Because I remember who I was.

And I remember how convinced I was that it was "different."

It wasn't different.

I was just hopeful.

Which is sweet.

But not sustainable.

Now?

I'm calm. I'm observant. I'm selective. I'm still soft. I'm just not negotiable.

And that's not bitterness.

That's calibration.

If someone wants chaos, they'll find it.

If someone wants clarity, they'll recognize it.

And me?

I'm not auditioning anymore. I'm not decoding blurred shoulders. I'm not romanticizing adrenaline. I'm not negotiating basic effort.

I survived a version of me who thought confusion meant depth.

She meant well.

She just confused intensity with intimacy and Wi-Fi with evidence.

I don't hate her.

I retired her.

Not angrily. Not dramatically.

Just... administratively.

And the calm version of me?

She doesn't chase clarity.

She selects it.

Afterword

If you're still thinking about them,
this didn't fail.

If you still have questions,
that doesn't mean you didn't grow.

You don't need closure
to move forward.

You just need enough truth
to stop going back.

And maybe that truth is simple:
It didn't work.
Not because you weren't enough.
But because it wasn't right.

And that has to be enough now.

www.ingramcontent.com/pod-product-compliance
Lightning Source LLC
Chambersburg PA
CBHW070805260726
48660CB00005B/1705